How to Talk About Jesus

With the Skeptics in Your Life

Ralph O. Muncaster

D1601127

HARVEST HOUSE PUBLISHERS

EUGENE, OREGON

Cover by Terry Dugan Design, Minneapolis, Minnesota

Harvest House Publishers, Inc., is the exclusive licensee of the federally registered trademark EXAMINE THE EVIDENCE Series.

A Special Thanks to Karen Bell-Wilcox for her endless hours spent contributing to the perspectives in this book and for her ministry contribution. Karen is a major leader in Strong Basis to Believe Ministries and has been involved in the research of several ministry topics. Karen is a CPA with a master's degree in business administration and has also pursued advanced studies in diverse areas of science.

By Ralph O. Muncaster

Can Archaeology Prove the New Testament?
Can Archaeology Prove the Old Testament?
Can We Know for Certain We Are Going To Heaven?
Can You Trust The Bible?
Creation vs. Evolution
Dinosaurs and the Bible
Does the Bible Predict the Future?
How Do We Know Jesus Is God?
How is Jesus Different from Other Religious Leaders?
How to Talk About Jesus With the Skeptics in Your Life
Is The Bible Really A Message From God?
Science—Was the Bible Ahead of It's Time?
What is the Proof For the Resurrection?
What is the Trinity?
What Really Happens When You Die?
Why Are Scientists Turning to God?
Why Does God Allow Suffering?

HOW TO TALK ABOUT JESUS WITH THE SKEPTICS IN YOUR LIFE
Examine the Evidence® Series

Copyright © 2001 by Ralph O. Muncaster
Published by Harvest House Publishers
Eugene, Oregon 97402

Library of Congress Cataloging-in-Publication Data

Muncaster, Ralph O.
   How to talk about Jesus with the skeptics in your life / Ralph O. Muncaster.
      p. cm. — (Examine the evidence series)
   Includes bibliographical references.
   ISBN 0-7369-0609-6
      1. Jesus Christ—Person and offices. I. Title.
BT202 .M84 2001
248'.5—dc21   00-046121

Printed in the United States of America.

04 05 06 07 08 09 / BP / 10 9 8 7 6 5 4

Contents

Why Is It Important to Tell Skeptics About Jesus?

The Importance of Discussing Jesus

Imagine that a "nutty professor" has invented a new pill that allows people to live two or three hundred years with the body of a 25-year old. Imagine he has given you a million pills and has told you to give them to a million people so they can have this amazing kind of life. But you have hidden them in your closet, giving *none* away, not even to your best friend, Joe.

Years have gone by. Joe has aged. Hair gray. Wheelchair. Wrinkles as deep as canyons. You're now both 94. Yet you are running marathons, staying up all night, looking 25 years old, happy as can be about the future. And you've never told anyone about the pills.

Wouldn't it be incredibly selfish and unloving for you not to tell others—even your best friend—about the greatest secret in life? (And wouldn't it be odd for your friend not to ask why your life has gone so well?)

This is the same as a Christian *not talking*, or a skeptic *not asking* about Jesus. But the difference is that Jesus can lead us to an eternal life with God—a life of supreme well-being—not a mere 300 years of "youth."

Christians, you know the "secret"—
skeptics don't! Talk with them!

Why Don't We Do It?

We talk with our friends about Buddha, Muhammad, Confucius, L. Ron Hubbard, Jim Jones, and other religious figures without fear. Why not Jesus?

Perhaps it's because He claimed to be the Son of God, and we know people will react differently when we mention Him. Perhaps it's because we don't feel qualified to talk about the evidence for the Bible, even though it's been successfully defended for centuries and is the only holy book verified by prophecy, history, archaeology, science, and the apparent sequence of creation.* Our fears about talking about Jesus are often unfounded. Furthermore, talking about Jesus is one of the most important things for Christians to do. (And for skeptics, it's just plain good sense to find out about Him.)

Christians have a strong reason to talk about Jesus—He commanded it (Matthew 28:19,20). Many Christians, however, are simply apathetic; they "already have their faith." Other times, Christians are afraid they will look like fanatics and lose their friends. Or they may fear embarrassment if their answers aren't good enough. However, tools and teaching exist today that can help Christians provide answers for the skeptics of the information age.†

It's a fact that skeptics are more interested in Jesus than ever. (For example, several of the bestselling issues of popular news magazines have had Jesus on the cover.) Skeptics often wonder about Jesus, but some of them may be afraid of getting into a deep, uncomfortable discussion. Others may be worried about being lured into some type of religious fanaticism. Or perhaps they fear that their peers might think of them as "strange." Yet in the back of most skeptics' minds are these nagging questions: "What if Jesus really *was* the Son of God? What would that mean to me?" The only way for them to find out is to ask questions—to investigate. *Christians and skeptics need to talk to one another.*

---

* See Notes and Bibliography for more sources.

† The *Examine the Evidence* series was designed to give Christians a resource for answering skeptics' questions, as well as to help skeptics themselves with issues about the Christian faith. See pages 43–46 for details about the entire series.

The Key Issues

SKEPTICS

1. Why is it so important to talk about Jesus? (See pages 10–13, 16–19, 22, 23, 46, 47.)

2. Is it worth the risk of embarrassment to ask about Jesus? (See pages 10–13, 20–23.)

3. How do I talk about Jesus without looking stupid (or strange)? (See pages 14, 15, 18–21.)

4. Can I talk to a Christian without being harassed? (See pages 14, 15, 24–27.)

5. What's in it for me? (See pages 10–13, 22, 23, 46, 47.)

Peace and Eternal Life

CHRISTIANS

1. Why is discussing Jesus so important? (See pages 10–13, 16–19, 22, 23, 46, 47.)

2. Can I approach others to talk about Jesus without being embarrassed? (See pages 10–13, 20–23, 32–37.)

3. Can I start to talk about Jesus without looking stupid (or strange)? (See pages 20, 21, 32–37.)

4. How do I help others feel comfortable about discussing Jesus? (See pages 38–41.)

5. What's in it for me? (See pages 10–13, 22, 23, 46, 47.)

Joy and Rewards

What Do We Mean by the Words "Skeptic" and "Christian"?

In this book, the term "skeptic" refers to anyone who has a barrier to believing and accepting God, the Bible, or Jesus Christ.

Level ## Basic Categories of Skeptics

7. *"Closed" hard-core skeptics*—Generally atheists, agnostics, or philosophers, this group is strongly against Jesus and the Bible, and often is opposed to any idea of a "God" as well. Their resistance is so strong that they will *never listen to reason.* Fortunately they are few in number. Jesus told His disciples not to spend their time with such obvious "rejectors" (Matthew 7:6; 10:14).

6. *"Open" hard-core skeptics*—Generally atheists, agnostics, or philosophers, this group is like the first except that they are open to listening to reason (I personally was once an open hard-core skeptic). This is a difficult group to talk with because they often have very intellectual arguments that may demand research and take a long time to discuss. It is easy to mistake them for closed skeptics.

5. *Apathetic skeptics*—These people are skeptics of God, Jesus, and the Bible who literally don't care. They are willing to accept life as it exists, along with any afterlife that may or may not be in store for them. The difficulty here lies in convincing these skeptics of the vast importance of knowing God—for both joy and peace on earth and the enormous eternal rewards. Barriers often need to be broken down before they will be open to even considering any true relationship with Jesus. Many skeptics fall into this category.

4. *Religious skeptics*—These people are involved in some type of non-Christian religion. If it is a cult (see insert on page 9), they are often highly indoctrinated into a social and economic system, which makes it difficult for them to listen to reason or to break free in any way. Even so, many members of cults or world religions have become Christians after investigating the evidence.

3. *General skeptics*—These are people who really don't know what they believe—they are simply skeptical about most things and see organized religion just as a group trying to get something out of them. Building strong trust first is vital to discussing Jesus with people in this group.

2. *Nonaffiliated skeptics*—This group has no real affiliation with any religion. They may identify themselves in a certain way—even as Christians—yet have made no real commitment to any person or theology. This is a very large group that can be very receptive to Jesus.

Christians—Use Care!

Many Christians have such a desire to help others find the power, love, and joy of Jesus that they push too hard. They seem fanatical and can be very offensive. Helping skeptics move a little closer to God should be our objective. Know when to stop!

Peter told us to be ready to defend our faith, but to do it with "gentleness and respect" (1 Peter 3:15).

1. *Seekers*—These people are genuinely interested in finding out about God—whether from a Christian or another perspective. It is vital that seekers hear the reasons for Christianity, especially since no other religion or holy book can meet the rigorous tests that God has included in the Bible.

How Do We Define a "Christian"?

(Skeptics: Know who to talk to about Jesus!)

The term "Christian" is extremely broad, and more often than not is used in a way that is not biblically based. For the purpose of this book, we will define a Christian by the following basic biblical factors. A Christian is someone who:

1. Believes there is a God who came to earth in the human form of Jesus (John 3:16; Romans 10:9).

2. Accepts God's free forgiveness of sin and gift of new life through the death and physical resurrection of Jesus (Ephesians 2:8-10; 1:7,8).

3. Switches to God's plan by being sorry for past wrongs and trying to do what's right (1 Peter 1:21-23; Ephesians 2:1-5).

4. Expressly makes Jesus the director of his or her life and asks for His guidance (Matthew 7:21-27; 1 John 4:15).

Jesus is both
Lord (CEO, Director)
and **Savior** (Source of eternal life)
for the Christian.

A Christian doesn't necessarily go to church every Sunday, have weekly Bible studies, and pray every day, though all of these things are good. Christianity is not based on rules. However, the Bible does tell us how to recognize a Christian.

How to Recognize a Christian

We can recognize those people who have truly accepted Jesus as both Lord and Savior by their "fruit" (actions or attitudes produced) as they grow spiritually (Matthew 7:16-20). The Bible describes what this "fruit" is:

"The fruit of the Spirit is love, joy, peace, patience, kindness, goodness, faithfulness, gentleness and self-control."
—Galatians 5:22,23

The Bible teaches that Christians *love God*, have an *intimate relationship with Jesus*, and *try to obey* His commands. Loving God means loving others—God's two greatest commandments (Mark 12:30,31). "Loving others" means that Christians should *want* to talk about Jesus (Matthew 28:19,20). (*A note to skeptics*: Look for Christians who *know* Jesus. They will want to talk to you!)

Skeptics Beware!

Many religions sound "Christian," yet have very unbiblical doctrine. The groups below are not Bible-based Christians:

- Church of Jesus Christ of Latter-Day Saints (Mormons)
- Jehovah's Witnesses
- Christian Scientists
- Unity School of Christianity
- The Unification Church ("Moonies")

Why Is Jesus So Important?

Knowing Jesus is tremendously important. He helps people deal with their past, their present and their future—for eternity. It is virtually impossible for anyone to even begin to understand the love, strength, and eternal rewards Jesus offers without talking about Him with others who know Him—with those who are true Christians.

The Past—Guilt and Resentment vs. Forgiveness

Psychiatrists, medical doctors, and professional counselors all agree that guilt, hatred, and resentment are among the leading causes of mental problems. This should be no surprise to anyone, since we see it all the time on the daily news. Hate crimes, murder, revenge, suicide—these and other dreadful things all flow from the evil human nature within us. The pressure is made worse by our consciences, which continually say to us, "What you are doing is wrong."

Through a new relationship with Jesus, however, we have the opportunity to be totally, 100-percent forgiven for all our past *and future* wrong choices (Matthew 12:31). Since God—not a human judge—is the ultimate authority in the matter of forgiveness of sins, when we put ourselves under the authority and guidance of Jesus and have a relationship with Him, we are forgiven for *all* wrongs. *All*—even murder, rape, and the sin God hates the most of all: pride. The only unforgivable sin is "blasphemy of the Holy Spirit," which means a *continual and ultimate rejection* of the Holy Spirit's prompting to accept God's greatest, most sacrificial gift: the life of His Son Jesus, who was crucified for our sins and is now resurrected (Mark 3:29).

The Present—Joy, Peace, and Hope

Jesus promised that, if we come to Him, we will find rest for our hearts and minds, and His burden will be light for us (Matthew 11:28-30). Why is this so? Consider this first—God created the universe, including the earth, human beings, and every other living creature. He knows the most intimate details of our design. His original plan was for humans to be obedient to Him, love

Him, and live with Him forever—just the same as His plan for the future after the end of time (Revelation 21:3). However, humans chose to disobey Him, which resulted in their spiritual death (separation from God) and eventually in physical death. Furthermore, the earth was cursed so that life for humans became painful and toilsome.*

But through the sacrifice and resurrection of Jesus, God made a way for human beings to have a *new relationship* with Him, a relationship through Jesus. Therefore, although Christians continue to live with the same difficulties that everyone else on earth does—daily problems, pain and suffering, the necessity of hard work—they can deal with the adversity better than other people, because they have been *reconnected* with God and have the power, love, and hope that He gives through Jesus, His Son.

This power, love, and hope have been demonstrated over many centuries. The authors of ancient non-Christian historical writings marveled at the joy expressed by Christians as they willingly accepted horrible executions for their faith. And anyone who has attended a true Christian's funeral knows that it is far from a morbid scene. Although grieving is natural (even Jesus wept over his friend Lazarus' death), the overall mood at a Christian's funeral is one of rejoicing, because the person who has died is now finally in the presence of God. Christians also seem to handle life's daily problems better. When they communicate frequently with God through prayer and trust that He is in control, their problems seem to produce less suffering than do similar problems for non-Christians.

The Future—Eternal Paradise with God vs. Hell

There is one issue involved in discussing Jesus that is by far the most important, yet it is the one least talked about. It is the matter of death, which leads to eternity (for Christians, an eternity in heaven with God). The Bible talks about this over and over again, but for some strange reason people now hate to discuss death

* See *Why Does God Allow Suffering?* in the *Examine the Evidence* series.

(this has been the case only since the late 1800s, about the time of Darwin). Yet death is inevitable! Not discussing it is like not talking about a tornado you know for certain will hit your town next year. Wouldn't any sensible person investigate options? Wouldn't any sensible person be prepared? Wouldn't any sensible person talk to experts in tornado survival?

Death is more certain than any tornado. Virtually all religions speak about death and offer some kind of hope for the afterlife, but the question is, *What is really true?* Many non-Christian religions offer attractive, "join-the-club" ways to gain a better afterlife, which makes them popular. Here are some examples.

- A *Mormon* man is promised a most attractive kind of paradise. He can be the god of his own planet, populating it with the progeny of heavenly sexual relations with his many wives. And the Mormon definition of hell differs greatly from the Scriptures (even though Mormons profess to honor and follow the Bible). To Mormons, "hell" as described in the Bible doesn't exist—it's simply a state of darkness for only the most evil non-Mormons.
- *Christian Scientists* believe that matter doesn't exist; that there is no sin and no hell. Since we are all sinless, there is no prospect of punishment if we don't choose God. (Presumably Hitler, Stalin, and every other evil person are equally perfect.) Everyone achieves fulfillment in a wonderful world of make-believe. (Note, however, that Christian Scientists still live life as though matter is real—for instance, they wouldn't deliberately jump off a 2000-foot cliff.)
- *Hindus* and the followers of some sects of *Buddhism* get continual chances to attain paradise (or nirvana) through repeated reincarnation. (However, for most people this requires thousands, even millions, of lives.)

We could add many more examples from other religions.[2] So, are Christians narrow-minded for rejecting ideas about the afterlife that don't come from the Bible? Jesus declared that He is "the way and the truth and the life. No one comes to the Father except through me" (John 14:6). His words are very specific.

Buddha is not the way, Muhammad is not the way, nor are any other people or religious leaders. Yes, Christianity is narrow-minded; perhaps the truth itself is narrow. Consider these things:

- The Bible is the only holy book that is confirmed by historical prophecy. It contains more than 600 predictions that have been historically fulfilled.
- Jesus is the only major religious leader who claimed to be God.
- Jesus is the only religious leader who has been raised from the dead.

A Relationship with Jesus Comes to Us Free

Jesus' incredibly wonderful promises come from God *completely free*. Forgiveness of the past, joy and peace in the present, and eternal paradise with God in the future—all free. What could be better? (See the steps on page 46.)

A Note About Non-Christian Religions

Many followers of non-Christian religions are sincere and perform good actions. Mormons, for example, are known for their emphasis on family life. Christian Scientists are known for their happiness. Many religions commend love, compassion, and moral behavior, and sometimes the earthly virtues of their followers seem to exceed those of real Christians.

However, keep in mind that only the Bible proves, through historical prophecy, that it is inspired by God. Choose your faith and your God wisely, because the final issue is *eternity*. Only if we are forgiven and have a relationship with God through Jesus can we live forever with God in paradise.

Those people who worship the wrong God or the wrong Jesus are already condemned (John 3:18), and if they do not turn to the real Jesus, they are doomed to suffer God's eternal anger—"weeping and gnashing of teeth" in hell (Matthew 13:42,50). Hell is forever. Seventy or even a hundred years of life on earth are nothing in comparison.

Perspectives on Discussing Jesus

A Skeptic's Perspective

Skeptics (as I once was) are reluctant to discuss Jesus. It's uncomfortable, it seems to border on fanaticism, and it just simply takes time.

Even so, many skeptics realize that a lot of people are convinced that Jesus is important. After all, why would magazines such as *Time, Newsweek,* and *US News & World Report* (not to mention many television programs) spend so much time discussing Him if He were "nothing"?

Apart from this, some skeptics also know that the Bible is by far the bestselling book of all time—not the Qur'an, *The Book of Mormon,* or the Egyptian Book of the Dead. That alone should lead many skeptics to at least read the Bible. Here are some of the thoughts and struggles of the skeptic:

A Skeptic Thinks—

- People who believe in Jesus are fanatics.
- The media tells us a lot about Jesus.
- Other people seem interested in Jesus.
- If Jesus comes up in a conversation, I might ask about Him.
- Otherwise, I'll accept life as is.

A Christian Thinks—

- We're normal. Jesus just gives us the way to know God.
- The media presents distorted views of Jesus.
- Many people are curious about Jesus, but few know Him.
- If Jesus comes up in a conversation, I'll talk about Him.
- Otherwise, I don't want to create an awkward situation.

A Skeptic's List of Objectives

1. Find out whether Jesus is real.

2. Find out whether the Bible was truly inspired by God.

3. Investigate whether Jesus really was resurrected from the dead, and if so, what that might mean to me.

4. Discover what I have to do to get into heaven or paradise.

5. Figure out what happens if I'm not "good enough."

Christians—Remember!
- Don't be self-righteous.
- Don't use "Christianese."
- Don't talk down to skeptics.

6. Develop a list of questions about Jesus that trouble me. Ask them.

7. If I come to believe that the Jesus of the Bible is real, ask "What's next?"

8. Find a Bible-based Christian and ask.

A Christian's Perspective

A Christian's aims in a discussion about Jesus are straight-forward: to make the skeptic *feel at ease* in talking about Jesus, and to help him *investigate or think for himself* about God, Jesus, and the Bible. Hopefully, the discussion will help the skeptic move closer to understanding Christianity. Sometimes Christians make the mistake of being far too aggressive and try to have a skeptic accept Jesus immediately. For skeptics in the "hard-core" category (see number 6 on page 7), this will not work. A direct approach may be effective if the person is a seeker or inquisitive skeptic (numbers 2 and 1 on page 8).

A Christian's List of Objectives

1. Help the skeptic learn that the Bible and Jesus are real, true, and historical.

2. Help the skeptic see that God inspired the Bible and that this can be proven through prophecy.

3. Help the skeptic learn the importance of Jesus' death and resurrection.

4. Share your personal story ("testimony").

5. Answer any questions as well as you can. (Research what you don't know.)

6. If he or she is ready, help lead the skeptic to Christ.

7. If he or she is not ready, suggest a follow-up meeting, or perhaps a church or group activity.

Why Is Jesus Different?

Christians are often asked, "Why is accepting Jesus as Lord and Savior the only way to establish a relationship with God? After all, there are many other founders of religions, who have many good ideas. How can they all be wrong?"

The Claims of Jesus

The claims of Jesus are very different from those of any other major founder of religion. Jesus maintained that He was *God incarnate*—God Himself existing as a human being. Evidence of Jesus making this claim abounds:

- Jesus stated, "I and the Father are one" (John 10:30).
- Jesus confirmed that He was the "king of the Jews" (meaning that He was the Messiah, the "anointed one" of God—see Matthew 27:11).
- Jesus accepted worship, which only God can rightly accept (Matthew 14:33; 28:9; John 9:38).
- Jesus forgave sins, which only God can do (Mark 2:5-10).
- Jesus accepted praise as the "king who comes in the name of the Lord" (Luke 19:37-40).

Confirmation of Jesus' Claims

Consider this: The ministry of Jesus lasted only about three years. That's not much time to build a foundation for a religion, especially in an era of no television, no telephones or e-mail, and slow travel. Nonetheless, it's abundantly clear that Jesus quickly became well-known and was accepted by many people as the true Son of God even before He was crucified; and the number of believers grew rapidly after His death and resurrection. Confirmation of Jesus' claims includes:

- Peter's declaration that Jesus was the Christ—the Messiah (Matthew 16:16).
- Stephen's affirmation, before he was stoned to death, that Jesus was the "Righteous One" who is at the right hand of God (Acts 7:51-60).
- Paul's change from an honored persecutor of Christians to a suffering follower of Jesus (Acts 9).

- Jesus' disciples, women who followed Jesus, and a man healed from blindness all worshiped Jesus—and the Jewish law reserved worship for God only (Matthew 14:33; 28:9; John 9:38).
- Jesus Himself confirmed His own deity by prophesying His death and resurrection with complete accuracy.

Jesus Rose from the Dead—Others Died and Remained in the Grave

It would be foolish not to recognize the uniqueness of someone who rose from the dead and then ascended to heaven without dying. There is vast evidence for and no evidence contrary to the resurrection of Jesus.[3]

- Jesus rose from the dead. To date, no other explanation has been put forward that can account for all the historical evidence.
- A multitude of historical documents report the resurrection as a historical fact. These documents include many very early manuscripts of the Gospels and apostolic letters.
- Archaeological finds attest to widespread belief in Jesus' resurrection among those people who lived *at the time of the event.*
- Buddha died and stayed dead. Joseph Smith died and stayed dead. Mary Baker Eddy died and stayed dead.
- The list goes on and on. Only Jesus rose from the dead. No one else has.

The Bottom-Line Conclusion

1. Jesus claimed to be God. No other founder of a major religion did.

2. Other people believed that Jesus was God—not just centuries later, but at the time. No other major religion's followers believed that their founder was God, though some founders were deified centuries after their lifetimes.

3. Jesus rose from the dead and ascended into heaven. No other founder did.

> Therefore, Jesus is very different from founders of other religions, and it is more important to learn about Him than about any other founder.

Investigating the Validity of the Evidence for Jesus

To investigate the validity of the manuscript evidence for Jesus, we need to go outside our typical methods for investigating events. Why? Because Jesus is so very different (of course, God is very different). Unfortunately, many instructors, reporters, and other investigators overlook the vast body of evidence documented *within the church* (which is the keeper of most documents) and turn to other sources such as the media, the encyclopedia, the Internet, or some group claiming to be "unbiased."

Some people might ask, "Aren't 'objective' sources more reliable than church history, since they are 'unbiased'?" The answer to this question is straightforward:

"Unbiased" sources are really very biased!
Any complete investigation demands analysis
of *both* sides of an issue.

Consider their motives. Many people who criticize the centuries of accumulated evidence for the Bible have a profit motive. Critics come from the world of academics and museums— philosophers, archaeologists, other scientists—who are concerned with prestige and money. (Ironically, these disciplines provide enormous support for Jesus and the Bible.)

So why do attacks on the Bible sell so well? Because people attack the truth when it makes them feel uncomfortable. (Attacks on other religions don't make the cover of *Time* magazine.) *The Bible is special.*

The Bible

On the other hand, the Bible is extremely unbiased. How do we know this?

1. The Bible records many unflattering events about God's people. A biased work would not report these.

2. The Bible has been challenged for thousands of years and still remains unmatched as a source of truth. It even survived extreme attempts to eradicate it. No other work compares to it—especially in its believability. And ever since it was first printed, it has been the world's bestselling book—by far.

3. Nearly all translations of the Bible go back as closely as possible to the original manuscripts. Present-day critics who make the front covers of *Time* and *Newsweek* and are featured on television specials presume that we—today—can better interpret the original accounts about Jesus than the people of His time. This is incredibly arrogant. (Would anyone claim, for instance, that we know more about the pyramids of Egypt than the ancient Egyptians did? We don't even know how they were built!) The early Bible manuscripts and other ancient supporting evidence about Jesus present much stronger testimony than any of today's theorists. Experts in courtroom evidence would agree.

How to Investigate Jesus—Whether You're a Christian or a Skeptic

1. Develop a list of questions about God, Jesus, and the Bible.

2. Ask God to reveal the truth (even if you don't think He exists—it can't hurt!), and recognize that He rewards those who seek Him (Hebrews 11:6).

3. Ask reliable people (see pages 8, 9) about their experience with and knowledge of Christianity.

4. Feel free to investigate other religions, but "test everything" (1 Thessalonians 5:21)

5. In any religion you research, make sure that there is *perfectly fulfilled, historical* prophecy.

6. Read books that present objective scholarship about the Bible (good books always include the Bible as a key reference—its accounts are highly accepted as history).

7. Focus on essentials, realizing that some questions may remain unanswered till later.

What if the Bible Is Wrong . . . or Right?

After having thought about the evidence on the previous pages, a skeptic might perhaps agree that investigating the claims of the Bible is important. Likewise, a Christian reader may now realize the importance of talking to skeptics. But let's ask this question again: Just how accurate is the Bible? Though the centuries of scrutiny it's undergone, along with the support it has from modern science, provide overwhelming cause to trust it, suppose the Bible is wrong? Or suppose it's right?

The skeptic might think, "I really have a hard time reading the Bible and believing its claims. On the other hand, what if the Bible is *right*? It would affect me forever! It would be stupid not to take a few hours (or days) to investigate it."

The Christian might think, "I have all the power that comes from knowing Jesus. My past is forgiven, my present is filled with love, joy, and peace, and I do many things to keep growing as a Christian. There's only one thing I'm uncomfortable with—talking to others about Jesus. Yet I know Jesus loves me and wants me to talk to others about His love."

Suppose the Bible Is Wrong

If a skeptic thoroughly investigates the Bible and determines that it is wrong, what has it cost him or her? Time. Yet since the Bible is considered an excellent resource on how to live by doctors, therapists, and others, this investment of time could nonetheless surpass the value of the best medical advice we could get about stress, relationships, security, and love.

> So any skeptic who reads the Bible and applies
> some of its principles can benefit greatly,
> whether or not the Bible is true!

The same holds true for Christians (if we use the definition of Christian from pages 8, 9). We can see in their lives incredible joy in the face of suffering, peace in difficult circumstances, love, hope, and many other benefits. If we consider the issue of divorce, for instance, some statistics from national polls seem to show that the divorce rate for "Christians" (that is, those who simply call themselves Christians) is nearly the same as the rate averaged for followers of all religions. However, when we look at married people who follow Jesus—meaning couples who go to church together, pray together, and read the Bible—their chance of divorce is much less.

Suppose the Bible Is *Right*

If the Bible is right, anyone who wants to can gain everything! By following a few simple steps, anyone can become part of the family of followers of Jesus Christ. By surrendering oneself to Him, believing and accepting His sacrifice and resurrection, and desiring to follow Him, anyone can receive 1) forgiveness of the past, 2) enjoyment of the present, and 3) assurance of an eternal future with God.

The Bible is also very clear about our freedom to choose against God and the consequences of that decision: eternal suffering in hell. Many people try to ignore the issue or pretend that hell doesn't exist. It does! Investigate the evidence while you can!

The Bible Says That God's Plan of Love Is Freely Available

There are no sign-up fees, no monthly dues, no mortgage payments—Jesus Christ and the wonderful things He brings into our lives are God's ultimate free gift, available to everyone. It seems like a deal "too good to be true," but it *is* true!

Why would anyone *not*
investigate the Bible?

The Importance of . . .

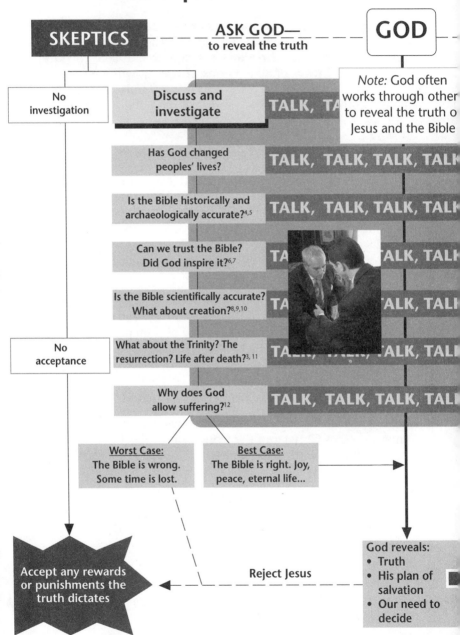

SKEPTICS

ASK GOD— to reveal the truth

GOD

Note: God often works through other to reveal the truth o Jesus and the Bible

No investigation

Discuss and investigate

TALK, TA

Has God changed peoples' lives?

TALK, TALK, TALK, TALK

Is the Bible historically and archaeologically accurate?[4,5]

TALK, TALK, TALK, TALK

Can we trust the Bible? Did God inspire it?[6,7]

TAALK, TALK

Is the Bible scientifically accurate? What about creation?[8,9,10]

TAALK, TALK

What about the Trinity? The resurrection? Life after death?[3,11]

TALK, TALK, TALK, TALK

No acceptance

Why does God allow suffering?[12]

TALK, TALK, TALK, TALK

Worst Case: The Bible is wrong. Some time is lost.

Best Case: The Bible is right. Joy, peace, eternal life...

Accept any rewards or punishments the truth dictates

Reject Jesus

God reveals:
• Truth
• His plan of salvation
• Our need to decide

. . . Talking About Jesus

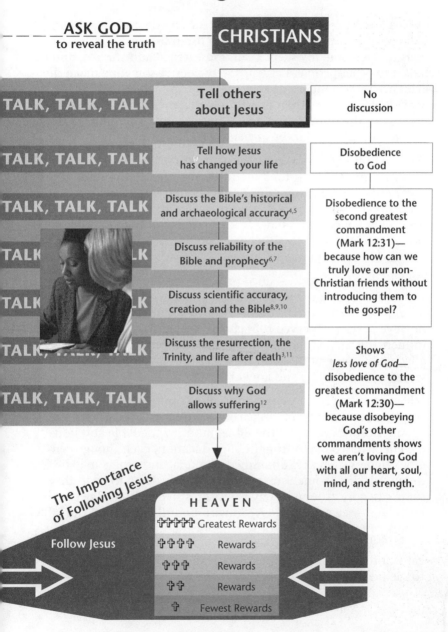

ASK GOD—
to reveal the truth

CHRISTIANS

TALK, TALK, TALK	**Tell others about Jesus**	No discussion
TALK, TALK, TALK	Tell how Jesus has changed your life	Disobedience to God
TALK, TALK, TALK	Discuss the Bible's historical and archaeological accuracy[4,5]	Disobedience to the second greatest commandment (Mark 12:31)— because how can we truly love our non-Christian friends without introducing them to the gospel?
TALK ...LK	Discuss reliability of the Bible and prophecy[6,7]	
TALK ...LK	Discuss scientific accuracy, creation and the Bible[8,9,10]	
TALK, TALK, TALK	Discuss the resurrection, the Trinity, and life after death[3,11]	Shows *less love of God*— disobedience to the greatest commandment (Mark 12:30)— because disobeying God's other commandments shows we aren't loving God with all our heart, soul, mind, and strength.
TALK, TALK, TALK	Discuss why God allows suffering[12]	

The Importance of Following Jesus

Follow Jesus

HEAVEN

✝✝✝✝✝	Greatest Rewards
✝✝✝✝	Rewards
✝✝✝	Rewards
✝✝	Rewards
✝	Fewest Rewards

The Skeptic's World

I was a skeptic for many years—almost as hard-core a skeptic as you might ever find (though I would listen to reason). It took me *years* to overcome my skepticism. I researched and studied, and I talked to other people. I asked, "Why doesn't someone make the evidence for the Bible's truth readily available to skeptics like me?" I needed more than just comforting preaching. I was a product of the information age; if I was going to commit myself to something, it had to be *factual*.

We don't often find a skeptic who pursues his or her investigation with such zeal. (It took me three years of intense study to become a Christian, something that shouldn't take so long. And it's risky—I could have died anytime before finishing my research.) But all skeptics have at least one major barrier to overcome—a barrier that usually has its origin in secular education, the media, or in apathy.

Skeptics live in a world shaped primarily by the influences with which they spend the most time—*school education, television, and other media,* such as the Internet. (In truly Christian households, however, I have observed that *parents* spend much more time influencing their children. These children seem to be much less affected by some of the typical elements in a skeptic's world: violence, hate, pride, and anger.)

School education has a tremendous effect on the shaping of a skeptic's patterns of thinking. The first textbook chosen for use in American schools was the Bible. But now the Bible and Jesus are effectively banned from public education, even though religious figures such as Muhammad, Buddha, and others may be discussed, since somehow they are not considered to be in the same category as Jesus. (Why is Jesus resisted so much? Because He is God—see pages 16, 17.) So with no influence from the Bible or talk of Jesus, and with only "theories" and other spiritual ideas to rely on, non-Christians actually develop a very biased, skeptical worldview from the time of early childhood. (This happened to me personally.)

Typical Components of a Skeptic's Worldview*

1. *Skeptics generally believe in no God, a limited God, or an unloving God (such as a "force").* Public schools and the media promote the theory of evolution. So do a vast number of scientists and academics, many of whom make a living by teaching it. Evolution tends to ignore new facts and implies that no God exists. A belief in a limited or unloving God comes from a skeptic's unawareness of God's nature.

2. *Skeptics tend to doubt many things that are in the Bible, especially miracles.* Objects of skepticism include the virgin birth of Jesus, the resurrection of Jesus, Jesus' ascension into heaven, Jesus' turning water into wine, the feeding of the multitudes, and many other supernatural events.

3. *Skeptics tend to "live for today."* They tend to not give thought to the future or whether eternity exists.

4. *Skeptics generally believe that morals are relative to the individual.* They conclude that if an action or attitude doesn't seem to hurt anyone else, then it's all right.

5. *Skeptics tend to place themselves first.* They often don't envision the joy of helping others, especially in the light of an eternal future.

The Language of Many Skeptics

Many skeptics—though not all—adopt the ideas and language of the culture. Here are some examples:

- "Morality is relative to what you believe."
- "Gotta watch out for Number One."
- "Do unto others as they did unto you."
- "Everyone else is doing it..."
- "The one who dies with the most toys wins."
- "If it feels good, do it."
- "It's just a little white lie."
- "If it doesn't hurt anyone, so what?"
- "Gotta keep up with the Joneses."

* Although these characteristics apply to many skeptics, they are generalizations. Skeptics' worldviews can vary greatly, so it's important to get to know people as individuals.

The Christian's World

The moment I became a Christian, there was no "bolt of lightning," no vision of God, and no sense of eternal peace (though all of this came later in some form). For me, becoming a Christian was a well-researched, well-thought-out decision. I had discussed my unbelief with other people, I had heard Christians' personal stories, and I had an absolute intellectual (and emotional) sense that knowing Jesus personally was the only true way of knowing God.

In the beginning my life changed gradually. Sometimes I still used offensive language and spoke thoughtlessly; I was still influenced by old ways of thinking; and, believe it or not, I was afraid of the Christian environment! Yet when I disobeyed God, my conscience gave me a sense of guilt. (This was new!) Things started changing for me.

It took a few years. Some non-Christian friends faded away. Other friends started to comment on how greatly I had changed—from self-centered to Christ-centered. My attitude

Christians—Think About the Impression You're Making

Christians have the same problems as everyone else—but they have been given God's life and help to deal with them. So don't act or sound self-righteous (after all, your righteousness comes from God, not from you). And try to avoid "Christianese." It's hard for skeptics to figure out what you mean by phrases like these:

- "Are you saved?"
- "God laid this on my heart."
- "Jesus is my rock."
- "I've been saved by the blood of the lamb."
- "Come join us for some fellowship."
- "You can have the power of the Holy Spirit."
- "God spoke to me."

about possessions changed—from seeking wealth to being content with what God provided me. I developed a passion to tell others about the truth of the Bible, which formerly I had not believed. Even in great difficulty, I was generally happy and was looking forward to the hope that God promises (Romans 8:28).

Gradually I was being transformed and transferred into the Christian world. It's not a world in which people feel superior to others—not a prideful world—it's a world in which people are actually accepted for who and what they really are (although there are churches that are exceptions). As time went on, I was changed inside—I *wanted* to do the will of God as expressed in the Bible. I *wanted* to go to church, to pray, to tap into a power and love much greater than my own. I realized that God was not only real, but far more accessible than I had believed or even imagined when I was a skeptic or a new Christian.

Major Components of a Christian's Worldview*

1. *Christians believe that God created the heavens and the earth and all life—without question!* This issue is so foundational that it alone brings many Christian parents to remove their children from public schools, not with the intent to "hide them," but to prepare them to build up their own faith and to be able to answer skeptics' questions.

2. *Christians believe that God is personal.* The Bible provides many examples of how God intervenes in the world to accomplish His will; many times He does this through people.

3. *Christians believe that God is holy, loving, and just.* These are three of the central characteristics of the God of the Bible.

4. *Christians believe they will spend eternity with God.* The Bible states this (Revelation 21:3).

5. *Christians tend to place others first.* In coming to earth, Jesus took on "the very nature of a servant" (Philippians 2:7), and Christians follow Him and His commands.

* This worldview varies only slightly among hundreds of Bible-based denominations.

Phase 1—Preparing to Talk About Jesus

1. **Pray for the truth to be revealed to the skeptic, and ask for the Holy Spirit's guidance for you.**

   Prayer is powerful. Prayers about any discussion should center around asking for a skeptic's "eyes to be opened" (2 Kings 6:17). It's also important to remember that God works through Christians, and that Jesus promised His disciples that the Holy Spirit would provide them with the right words to say (Luke 12:12).

2. **Learn basic answers to the most obvious questions.**

   Some of the most common questions are 1) Why does God allow suffering? 2) How can we explain creation when scientists say evolution is fact? 3) How do we know the Bible is inspired by God? 4) Is the Bible historically accurate? 5) How do we know the manuscripts for the Bible have not changed? (The *Examine the Evidence* series has been developed to help with this basic information—see pages 43–46.)

   If you study the evidence for just the most common points above, you will be well-prepared to talk about Jesus. Answers to more complex questions are readily available as well.

   ## How I Moved from Skepticism to Christianity

   I was once very arrogant and was certain that only ignorant people believed the Bible. One day, a Christian suggested some evidence for its truth and *challenged me* to investigate it. (Sometimes only a small seed of information is necessary.)

   I was amazed! Fact after fact—from history, archaeology, records about Jesus, manuscript reliability, science, and creation—agreed with the biblical account. I was stunned. Was everything I had learned from school and the media about the Bible wrong? I labored over large volumes, went to seminars, had personal discussions—and finally I accepted Jesus.

3. **Develop trust and a sincere relationship with anyone you approach.**

   This does not necessarily mean a long-term effort to become close friends. A relationship and a degree of trust can be built in about ten minutes, depending on the situation. This can be done at Little League fields, on airplanes, at company picnics, and in many other situations. The key is to be sincerely interested in a skeptic's life, to be humble, and to be *yourself* (not a "Bible-beating evangelist").

4. **Know the skeptic's "world" (see pages 24, 25), and know when to back off.**

   Remember, many skeptics fear a pushy Christian who will throw a lot of "Bible knowledge" at them and try to pressure them into Christianity. *To skeptics, the Bible is not true.* It is better to start where they are, in the secular world—using examples that tie into biblical truth (like the life of Jesus). Then issues can be discussed. But be sensitive to voice tone and body language—*know when to stop.*

5. **Follow up.**

   Without making a skeptic feel uncomfortable, try to find some follow-up opportunity. A later discussion, an invitation to church, a book given to the person with an appointment to discuss it, or a group meeting on a topic of both secular and Christian importance—all of these are good follow-up ideas.

Things to Consider

1. **You may start praying long before you actually talk to someone you are thinking about.**

   But eventually the topic of God, Jesus, or the Bible will come up. At that point, it's important to encourage the other person to pray for the truth. It will seem strange for an atheist or agnostic to pray to a "God" he or she doesn't believe in. But just encourage the person to pray something like this:

"God, I don't know if You're real or not.
But if You are, I pray that You will reveal to me
the truth of Your existence and a true path
to get to know You better."

2. **Spend some time learning where to find evidence supporting the Bible.**

If you know that someone you want to help has specific barriers, research those issues. (The *Examine the Evidence* series was designed for just such a purpose. It answers the basic questions in a simple, persuasive format. There are also excellent in-depth resources listed in the bibliographies for anyone wishing to pursue a subject further.) You don't need to know all the answers. Just know where to find them.

Some churches and organizations offer classes or programs to help Christians explain their faith. These can be very helpful, especially when they give attendees a chance to practice skills in talking about Jesus. I have seen amazing results from teaching this approach at churches and colleges.

3. **Because Jesus, God, and the Bible are such sensitive issues, you must first establish *trust*.**

Suppose you are sitting beside a total stranger at a Little League game. Within about ten minutes, you can learn a lot by listening to him or her talk about his or her life, child, and feelings, though sometimes it takes longer. In the course of the conversation, it is easy to bring up some relevant fact that ties the Bible into the person's secular interest (for example, the "Mars rock," the discovery of the "Cyrus cylinder," the "Dead Sea scrolls," the "punctuated equilibrium" theory of creation). You don't have to know the above terms; just know a few facts that relate the Bible to the world and Jesus. (The ministry of Strong Basis to Believe is evidence of how our current information-based society responds to a fact-based approach to the Bible. But note: Your personal story is still one of the best ways to approach many people.)

4. **Many skeptics get nervous when the conversation turns to God, Jesus, and the Bible.**

   If you detect a conversational roadblock, such as a sudden change in topic, a turn away from you to another person, or any other verbal or body-language signal, back off! There might be a future opportunity for more conversation, but a pushy Christian can do more harm than good.

5. **Follow-up is not as hard as it might seem.**

   If an interesting conversation about any biblical-secular topic occurs and the beginning of a relationship develops, it's not difficult to set up a future meeting or even invite someone to church or to hear a speaker who might be discussing that topic.

Phase 2—Starting a Discussion About Jesus

1. **Look for opportunities.**

   Opportunities arise when you least expect them (see insert on page 42). As Peter said, "Always be prepared to give an answer" for the hope that lies within you (1 Peter 3:15).

2. **Build trust and a relationship.**

   People generally resist talking about religion with people they don't know. But building a basic relationship doesn't always take much time. Christians can ask other people about their lives, listen to them, and find out things that can lead to a question about the secular world and the Bible. (Jesus always started where people were at in their lives.)

3. **Ease into a conversation.**

   Often a newsworthy event (for example, the "Mars rock") or some reading that you've done can be the basis for launching into a discussion about the Bible. Be sure to know some facts.

4. **Listen.**

   Especially when Christians are knowledgeable, they tend to talk more than listen. Listening is the key to understanding a skeptic's beliefs and barriers.

5. **Answer questions and follow up.**

   Christians will be able to answer some questions; some they may not be able to answer. But in any case, there should be a follow-up session to talk about issues you've researched and to further the discussion.

Be Prepared. Be Bold.

Once they're prepared, Christians will be amazed at the impact they can have.

I was asked to help out at a lecture by Michael Behe (author of *Darwin's Black Box*) that was given at UCI (The University of California, Irvine). The university is highly respected in biochemistry. Right after Behe's lecture, I was told that a UCI biochemistry professor had brought in a large group of students to denigrate Behe's position (Behe proposes that evolution is impossible).

In the back, I raised my hand and asked the professor to ignore Behe for just a moment and to try to explain the problem of chirality. ("Chirality" is the term for the observed phenomenon that all amino acids in DNA are of the same molecular orientation. This is vital to the making of DNA—and its origin by chance is mathematically impossible to explain.)[8,9]

The professor began by stating that there was an enormous body of evidence supporting the chance origin of chirality. I asked him to provide one name, one journal article, one piece of hard evidence about the overcoming of the chirality problem. He repeated that there was enormous evidence. So I again asked him to produce one example...there was no response. And again I asked him. (I knew that this had been a "mathematically impossible" problem for decades—perhaps he felt his status alone was enough to intimidate me.) He couldn't provide any evidence and eventually walked away embarrassed. Students then turned to me, asking questions. With the Holy Spirit, sometimes one issue is enough.

The point is not that I was anyone special—the professor was the expert. The point is that a few solid facts can expose misrepresentation of the Bible and false thinking.

Skeptics' Basic Attitudes

Many Christians feel that it's hard to approach the skeptics in their lives. But with a few guidelines and some basic understanding, it's really not difficult. One thing that is important to understand is some of the common attitudes that you will encounter when starting a discussion with skeptics. Remember that each attitude offers potential opportunities.

1. *Inquisitive*—This is the easiest kind of skeptic to relate to. Inquisitive skeptics ask questions. They are seeking something; often, it is they who approach you. They want to believe, but have some barriers that need discussion and explanation. Sometimes they need reassurance that Christianity is actually working for someone they trust. If you take the following steps, it's easy to connect with inquisitive skeptics:

   • *Let them talk* about their issues and questions; listen to them carefully.

   • *Relate to them* with your own story or someone else's.

   • *Tell your own story* (your "testimony") about what Jesus has done in your life.

   • *Address any barriers* with answers, a follow-up meeting, or with resources that skeptics can read or view.

   • *Let them know you care* about them. This often opens the door to follow-up.

2. *Aggressive*—This type of skeptic attacks Christianity and the Bible. Oddly enough, aggressive skeptics are usually easier to deal with than passive ones (see number three below). Why? Because at least they care enough to talk and often are willing to accept good answers. Often they come to you—they may hear you talking to someone else about Jesus, see you reading a Bible, or hear you stand up for the Christian worldview at a public event. The following steps are generally effective in approaching aggressive skeptics:

   • *Make sure they define their position* about their problem or issue. Aggressive skeptics often win support with senseless rhetoric that can easily be challenged.

- *Keep a loving attitude,* even under attack. This is strong evidence of the reality of Christianity.
- *Ask questions* so that you can fully understand aggressive skeptics' worldview, their barriers to Christianity, and most important, what evidence they have to support it! This last point is vital, because some of the most esteemed voices that speak against Christianity have *no hard evidence* to support their contentions. Christians often fail to demand evidence because they feel intimidated (see insert on page 33). And don't just settle for "theories."
- *Be specific about your own evidence* on the subject. If you don't know anything about the subject, set up a future meeting and then research it. The Bible is true; the evidence exists. You may not know the evidence yet, but you can certainly find it.
- *Thank skeptics for their interest* (no matter how heated the conversation). Again, this will testify to the reality of Christianity. Your credibility will be strengthened after skeptics have seen how you respond under stress.

Note that, although now you may be afraid of dealing with aggressive skeptics, this fear will subside with time and experience.

3. *Passive*—Though on the surface it seems easy to deal with passive skeptics, people who are passive and apathetic are actually very difficult to approach about God, Jesus, or the Bible. Essentially, they don't care one way or another (see Jesus' words about the danger of "lukewarmness"—Revelation 3:14-22). In order to start a meaningful conversation with passive skeptics, your words or actions need to bring them to the point of "caring."

- *Discuss a topic of concern,* such as someone's death, or a drug or violence problem.
- *Engage their thinking*—"What if this happened to you?"
- *Reveal how you would cope* by giving a story (a "testimony") about how Jesus helped you in your life.
- *Suggest to them that finding the right authority for life is critical.* Tell them how you found the Bible and came to trust it for your life.

Examples of Starting a Discussion

Here are some examples of how to initiate a discussion about the Bible with each type of skeptic:

1. *With an inquisitive skeptic*—You are on a business trip with a co-worker, and after some small talk your friend says, "I understand you're a Christian. You know, I've always wondered how people believe all that stuff about a virgin birth and a resurrection of someone from the dead. How do *you* believe all that?"

   You reply, "Personally, I've never had a problem believing it, because soon after I started praying and really getting to know Jesus, I started to see miracle after miracle take place in my own life. I'll give you examples if you'd like. However, I also know of others who had trouble with the issue of miracles the way you do, yet still came to believe in the miracles of the Bible. Why do you believe that miracles are impossible?"

   The benefits of this approach: 1) You brought in personal testimony about your skeptic friend's barriers to belief, thus opening the door for future discussion; 2) You related to the skeptic in his or her own world ("I know of others who had trouble with the issue"); 3) You prompted the skeptic to give more information to continue the discussion.

2. *With an aggressive skeptic*—You're talking about the Bible with a friend at the beach when a bystander interrupts: "You Christians think you know it all. There's no reason to think you're any more 'right' than any other religion is!"

   You reply: "It's *great* to hear someone who's not afraid to talk about God and to try to figure out if there are any differences between religions. What approach did you take to decide that all religions are the same?"

   The benefits of this approach: 1) You helped the skeptic feel at ease in talking about God; 2) Your reply wasn't defensive, and it communicated that investigation of religions was the right thing to do, thus supporting the skeptic's boast; 3) You gently asked how he or she approached supporting the claim—which provided an excellent springboard for further discussion.

3. *With a passive skeptic*—You are at a Little League game when an acquaintance you've often seen before takes his usual place beside you at the fence. You haven't exchanged many words in

> ## Know When to Stop!
>
> Any of the approaches in these examples can work, depending on the circumstances. But be alert for signs that the person you're talking with is uncomfortable. Your next step should be to try to arrange a follow-up meeting as soon as possible.

the past, but you know he's a high school science teacher and has some family problems. After some small talk—"Great play your son just made! Have you started to look for an agent for him yet?...By the way, I was reading about the 'Mars rock,' and we were talking about it in a men's group I go to. You're a scientist—do you think there's life on other planets?"

To continue the discussion—Bring up creation, God, life after death, the probability of the random evolution of life, the scientific accuracy of the Bible, or any other such topic.

The benefits of this approach: 1) You made your skeptic acquaintance feel at ease by not introducing God, the Bible, or religion at the outset. Those topics were normal follow-ups from the first part of your conversation. 2) You started out in the skeptic's area of interest, then naturally raised a more important eternal issue. 3) You could easily propose a follow-up discussion or invitation to an activity, since the issues you discussed are complex, and the skeptic needs to be encouraged to pursue them.

Answering Questions—It's Important to Know Some Facts[13]
(See pages 28, 30, 43–46)

Recently conducted research indicated the following: 1) 85 percent of "active" Christians wished they were better prepared for discussing Jesus; 2) only 13 percent of skeptics became Christians through church alone; 3) over half of the Christians surveyed believed not in the biblical Jesus and the Bible's teaching—but that being a "really good person" could get someone to heaven.[13]

Bottom Line: Christians need to be prepared to give accurate answers. (This is what the *Examine the Evidence* series is intended to help teach.)

Phase 3—Discussing Jesus Comfortably

1. **Allow the skeptic to talk and explain his or her barriers to belief.**

   Everyone likes to be heard; few people like to listen. When it comes to the delicate situation of exploring the evidence for Jesus, listening is critical. Try to understand where skeptics are coming from (as Jesus did).

2. **Be patient. Think of moving someone *closer* to Jesus, not necessarily all the way.**

   Research shows that effective relationships with Jesus are built over time.[13] So be prepared to engage in more than one conversation if possible. However, recognize that circumstances sometimes prevent a long-term relationship and that "planting a seed" can be very powerful (see insert on page 42).

3. **Look for an opportunity to share your personal experience.**

   Research[13] shows that your personal relationship with Jesus is one of the most powerful influences you can have on others (see insert below). Develop your story[11] (a compact way of telling your experience).

Preparing Your Personal Story
(Your "Testimony")

One of the most effective means of helping others understand what a relationship with Jesus can be is to discuss your own personal story.

Some preparation is necessary, and it's good to have both a short (one-minute) version and a long (five-minute) version. Since you never know ahead of time what length might be appropriate.

To be effective, you should include the following points:

1. What your life was like before you knew Jesus.

2. What caused you to consider Jesus.

3. How your life has changed since accepting Him.

Note: Research indicates that steady communication about Jesus with families and friends is one of the most effective methods to help others come to know Him.[13]

---

4. **Determine the biggest roadblocks.**

   Every non-Christian has at least one basic barrier to belief in Jesus. It's important to determine what it is in order to discuss it and, hopefully, answer any questions.

5. **Answer as many questions as possible and set up a follow-up discussion.**

   Research indicates that most of us who are Christians are not trained to know our faith as well as we should be, and furthermore are not equipped to answer questions (see insert on page 37). We should do the best we can, research the questions, and get back to skeptics as soon as possible.

Developing Your Testimony

A "testimony" is a *story* about your life (to skeptics, the word "testimony" is either "Christianese" or "legalese," whereas a "personal story" is just telling about yourself). To develop your personal story, think about describing your life to a close friend. Your story has a beginning (your life before Jesus), a middle (finding Jesus), and an end (life with Jesus). It's very straightforward.

Short testimonies often provide the best openings for questions that lead to in-depth discussions. A 15-second testimony might go this way: "I grew up in an abusive family and experienced pain during childhood. I felt as though things were always my fault. I was angry. I hated other people. One day, a guy on the basketball court told me how Jesus had changed his life; I wanted what he had. He told me how to follow Jesus. My life has been so happy ever since then."

Elements of a Good Short Testimony

- It must be truthful (not exaggerated or embellished).
- It must be sincere and personal.
- It should start from a point that a skeptic can relate to.
- It must be passionate (it must engage the hearer's mind *and* heart).
- It must tell about a change that Jesus has made in you.
- It must give the glory to God.
- It must not "preach" or be self-righteous.
- It should encourage follow-up questions or conversation.

What Can Longer Testimonies Do?

- They can relate elements of your personal story that are specifically applicable to the person you're talking to.
- They allow you time to describe God's long-term, slowly unfolding miracles in your life.
- They can be more believable by giving your hearer more details and evidence to consider.

My One-Minute Testimony

I grew up in a home where we went to church every week but didn't ever talk about God, Jesus, or the Bible at home. So I came to believe that all "real" facts were learned in school, not at church or at home.

Going on through life, I thought I was successful. I held prestigious positions at Fortune 500 firms, earned lots of money, and had a great deal of "power." But no matter how far I got, even to the highest levels of management— with wealth beyond my dreams—nothing was enough. I was not really happy, and I traveled about 200,000 miles a year—away from my family. If someone mentioned Jesus or the Bible, I'd smile at the other person's "stupidity." I was very arrogant.

One day, I was challenged to research the Bible and was told I would find all of it to be true. I realized I had nothing to lose and maybe something to gain, since I knew that the Bible talked about joy on earth and eternal life.

Everything I researched in the Bible turned out to be true. History, science, and prophecy all demonstrated that the Bible contained insight from God. I was astounded—I couldn't believe I'd never heard facts like these before. I committed my life to following Jesus.

There was no "lightning bolt" or vision. In fact, personal disaster hit me almost immediately after I became a Christian. But my new faith got me through extremely difficult circumstances that I now realize could have brought me to kill myself. And as time went on, I found enormous peace and joy.

Now I ask God daily to direct my life. Never have I felt so much contentment. Never so much love. All the "trappings" of the past are gone. I'm happy, and I'm looking forward to eternity.

Phase 4—Deciding What to Do Next

1. **Determine at what stage the skeptic is in his or her thinking.**

   As a conversation with a skeptic draws to a close, it's important to assess the situation. What is the skeptic thinking? Is there a major unanswered question? Are there other problem areas? If so, what are they? Were you able to share your personal story? The main aims at the close of an encounter are: first, to figure out what main roadblocks still remain; and second, to suggest a nonthreatening means of continuing a relationship—perhaps a lunch, an invitation to an event, or just "see you next week."

2. **Offer the skeptic help (do not force it) in discovering answers to his or her questions.**

   Skeptics often don't ask for help. Why? Because they fear a commitment to a religious group or to a line of thinking they don't yet accept. Any offer of help needs to be sincere and include follow-up.

3. **Assist with materials.**

   Christians often don't know which resources to select in order to help other people. On pages 43–46 you can find a list of other books in the *Examine the Evidence* series. They are designed to help skeptics, and they can help you answer most questions that skeptics will ask you. Each book also has a bibliography that suggests sources for further study.

4. **Invite the skeptic to church or another event.**

   Although research indicates that church alone does not help many people accept Jesus (see insert on page 37), it does play an important part in helping people understand God.[13]

5. **Assure the skeptic you are not a "threat."**

   Your words, tone of voice, and body language can assure a skeptic you've become acquainted with that you are a friend who's interested in his or her well-being, not a religious fanatic.

An Example: Planting Seeds While Traveling

One time, while waiting to board an airplane in Chicago, I experienced a typical string of delays and cancellations because of bad weather. A woman sitting next to me in the waiting area asked me why I was so engrossed in the book I was reading—which happened to be the Bible. I told her that I researched it; she simply replied that she never believed any of its stories.

I left the area to phone the people who were expecting me in Dallas. Upon returning, I boarded, found my seat, and noticed that the only empty seat on the plane was the one next to me. Then I saw the woman I'd met in the waiting area struggling down the narrow aisle, and I realized she was heading for the only seat available—beside me. At first my heart sank, since I had hoped to sleep, and I now saw that this flight was going to be taken up by conversation. But then I shook off my concern for myself and began to think how incredibly more important it was to help someone find Jesus than to sleep. God had placed this woman next to me for a reason.

For the next three hours I was bombarded with questions: How do we know Jesus is real? That the Bible is inspired by God? That it hasn't been altered since it was written? That it's accurate? What's the "proof"?

As the conversation went on, the woman's heart softened, and she became more receptive. In the course of one plane flight, she had changed from a hard-core skeptic to a seeker. She asked how to become a Christian. Though she was too nervous to do so yet, I gave her some books and told her how to do it whenever she was ready.

Slightly later, while I was waiting for the rental car shuttle van, I saw a woman stumbling down a broken escalator with a load of heavy bags. I risked missing the van in order to jog up the steps and help her. It turned out to be the same woman again! Seeds were planted that day—and with God's help, they'll grow.

The *Examine the Evidence* Series Is Designed for Skeptics

The *Examine the Evidence* series is based on the
author's journey to Christianity.

As a hard-core skeptic, I found it difficult to find answers about religion. Both Christians and followers of nearly every other religion told me to rely on "faith" (blind faith). I didn't buy it. It seemed to me that...

...If there was a *single God* of the entire universe,
He, She, or It would obviously leave evidence of a *single truth*.
Otherwise, anyone could make any kind of
argument for "faith" in any god.
Research helped me discover that evidence.

The Background of the Series

I was a product of the information age—well-educated, wanting facts easily and quickly, and believing in virtually all secular viewpoints, especially the theory of evolution. I thought that Christians (and followers of other religions) were mere fanatics whose beliefs were unsupported. Like most people today, *I didn't want to spend a lot of time to have my questions answered, and I was very skeptical if I couldn't have "hard facts."* But the Christians I spoke to had no answers for the faith within them. And there was no single book or text available that could give precise, thoroughly researched answers to my questions. It was a dilemma. Either I could give up—or start a lengthy process of research. Knowing that my eternal future could be in the balance, I decided to start intensive research of Christianity and other religions.

Though I don't recommend this lengthy process for anyone (since any of us could die today), it took me three years of research and three cover-to-cover readings of the Bible, as well as reading other holy books, to be certain the God of the Bible was the one real God—and to accept Jesus Christ. I had to address many issues: Is the Bible historically accurate? Were the manuscripts translated correctly? Do science and the Bible line up with each other? and so on. After I found that the Scriptures were accurate in these areas, the final convincing "proof" to me was the *precise prophecy* in the Bible. My three-year research of Christianity, along with many other years of study and research, is represented in the *Examine the Evidence* series; I hope to make it a lifelong work to bring the facts to a skeptical world—with Christians as "God-called" messengers.

During my early years of research, it became apparent that...

...most Christians didn't know the basis for their faith.
...most Christians couldn't answer the questions of skeptics.
...no quick-to-understand materials existed to present the truth.

The ministry of Strong Basis to Believe was started in 1991 at Saddleback Church in the Los Angeles, California, area. Rick Warren, the church's senior pastor, suggested that I establish the ministry to help provide skeptics with answers about the Christian faith, either directly or through Christian friends or acquaintances. Continual requests for information that would help with these answers led to the development of the *Examine the Evidence* series. Now Strong Basis to Believe has expanded beyond Saddleback Church to hundreds of organizations worldwide.

Using the *Examine the Evidence* Series

The *Examine the Evidence* series was developed to answer the most frequently asked questions that Strong Basis to Believe has encountered over the last ten years. The subjects are broken down into easy-to-digest "bite-sized" books that use inserts, charts, and special layouts to make issues easy to understand. They are especially helpful to Christians who want to learn answers to typically asked questions; they are also very useful to help skeptics overcome specific barriers to belief.

Each book is tailored to a specific area of investigation. Once you determine the most basic barriers, the following books can help you discuss the issues with your skeptic friend or acquaintance; or you can give the books to a skeptic directly (they were designed for skeptics, as I once was).

- **Does God exist? Do we know whether God inspired the Bible?**

  Does the Bible Predict the Future? and *Is the Bible Really a Message from God?* review many of the 600-plus historical prophecies in the Bible. One-hundred-percent accurate historical prophecies are unique to the Bible; they confirm that it was inspired by God and that God in fact exists. *Science—Was the Bible Ahead of Its Time?* and *Creation vs. Evolution* demonstrate that the Bible contains many scientific facts that were not discovered by scientists until centuries after the Bible manuscripts were written. They also show the Bible is completely accurate—as far as today's science can confirm—in the scientific information it contains.

- **Is the Bible historically accurate? Does archaeology support the Bible?**

  How Do We Know Jesus Is God?, *What Is the Proof for the Resurrection?*, and *What Really Happened on Christmas Morning?* are all similar in that they provide information about the historicity of Jesus. Each book deals with different events in Jesus' life. Further confirmation of the historical accuracy of the Bible can be found in *Can Archaeology Prove the Old Testament?* and *Can Archaeology Prove the New Testament?* These two books provide "hard evidence" from archaeological research that supports the information contained in the Bible.

- **Is the Bible we have today accurate? Were the right books selected?**

  Can You Trust the Bible? deals with the Bible manuscripts themselves and shows how archaeological finds of manuscripts—documents that we can see and touch today—confirm the accurate transmission of the original writings into the Bible we have today. It also recounts many details of how the Bible came into existence, disproving claims that the Bible was dishonestly conceived or was somehow changed over the course of the centuries; and it tells us why we can trust the manuscripts and translations we have today as accurate representations of the original manuscripts.

- **Is there concealed evidence in the Bible? What about life after death?**

  Are There Hidden Codes in the Bible? looks at a current idea concocted by some authors that the Bible has mysterious "hidden codes." These "codes" are specifically shown to be false. However, the book does demonstrate that the Bible contains "concealed evidence" that is abundant and readily understandable—just as Jesus stated.

What Really Happens When You Die? addresses the many questions—asked and unasked—that people have about death and life after death.

- **Why does God do what He does? What makes Him unique?**

  Why Does God Allow Suffering? clarifies God's purposes in allowing suffering and discusses how it fits into His overall plan to redeem everyone to Him. *How Is Jesus Different from Other Religious Leaders?* spotlights Jesus in comparison with founders of the world's largest religions and Christian cults.

- **Do some people go to heaven, and others don't? How do we know?**

  Can We Know for Certain We Are Going to Heaven? provides evidence of the existence of a heavenly realm and assurance that it will be an eternal state for all those who come to God through Jesus Christ.

Common Questions

How Can We Ensure the Right Relationship So We Can Go to Heaven?

When Jesus said that not all people who use His name will enter heaven (Matthew 7:21-23), He was referring to people who think that using Christ's name along with rules and rituals is the key to heaven. A *relationship* with God is not based on rituals and rules. It's based on grace, forgiveness, and on having the right standing with Him through Jesus Christ.

How to Have a Personal Relationship with God

1. **B**elieve that God exists and that He came to earth in the human form of Jesus Christ (John 3:16; Romans 10:9).

2. **A**ccept God's free forgiveness of sins and gift of new life through the death and resurrection of Jesus Christ (Ephesians 2:8-10;1:7,8).

3. **S**witch to God's plan for your life (1 Peter 1:21-23; Ephesians 2:1-7).

4. **E**xpressly make Jesus Christ the director of your life (Matthew 7:21-27; 1 John 4:15).

Prayer for Eternal Life with God

"Dear God, I believe You sent Your Son, Jesus, to die for my sins so I can be forgiven. I'm sorry for my sins, and I want to live the rest of my life the way You want me to. Please put Your Spirit in my life to direct me. Amen."

Then What?

People who sincerely take these steps become members of God's family of believers. A new world of freedom and strength is available through Jesus' life within you, expressing itself through prayer and obedience to God's will. This new relationship can be strengthened by taking the following steps:

- Find a Bible-based church that you like and attend regularly.
- Set aside some time each day to pray and read the Bible.
- Locate other Christians to spend time with on a regular basis.

God's Promises to Believers

For Today

"Seek first His kingdom and His righteousness,
and all these things [things to satisfy all your needs]
will be given to you as well."
—*Matthew 6:33*

For Eternity

"Whoever believes in the Son has eternal life,
but whoever rejects the Son will not see life,
for God's wrath remains on him."
—*John 3:36*

Once we develop an eternal perspective, even the greatest problems on earth fade in significance.

Notes

Note: Titles with an asterisk are excellent tools to help you prepare to talk about Jesus.

1. Zodhiates, Spiros, *The Complete Word Study of the Old Testament*, Chattanooga, TN: AMG Publishers, 1994.
2. McDowell, Josh, *Handbook of Today's Religions*, San Bernardino, CA: Campus Crusade for Christ, 1983.
3. Muncaster, Ralph O., *What Is the Proof for the Resurrection?* Eugene, OR: Harvest House, 2000.*
4. Muncaster, Ralph O., *Can Archaeology Prove the New Testament?* Eugene, OR: Harvest House, 2000.*
5. Muncaster, Ralph O., *Can Archaeology Prove the Old Testament?* Eugene, OR: Harvest House, 2000.*
6. Muncaster, Ralph O., *Can You Trust the Bible?* Eugene, OR: Harvest House, 2000.*
7. Muncaster, Ralph O., *Does the Bible Predict the Future?* Eugene, OR: Harvest House, 2000.*
8. Muncaster, Ralph O., *Creation vs. Evolution*, Eugene, OR: Harvest House, 2000.*
9. Muncaster, Ralph O., *Creation vs. Evolution* (videotape), Eugene, OR: Harvest House, 2000.*
10. Muncaster, Ralph O., *Science—Was the Bible Ahead of Its Time?* Eugene, OR: Harvest House, 2000.*
11. Muncaster, Ralph O., *What Really Happens When You Die?* Eugene, OR: Harvest House, 2000.*
12. Muncaster, Ralph O., *Why Does God Allow Suffering?* Eugene, OR: Harvest House, 2001.*
13. Barna, George, *10 Myths about Evangelism* (audiotape), Ventura, CA: Gospel Light, 1996.

Bibliography

Note: Titles with an asterisk are excellent tools to help you prepare to talk about Jesus.

Elwell, Walter A. (Editor), *Evangelical Dictionary of Theology*, Grand Rapids, MI: Baker Book House Co., 1984.

Geisler, Norman, and Brooks, Ron, *When Skeptics Ask*, Grand Rapids, MI: Baker Books, 1990.*

Life Application Bible, Wheaton, IL: Tyndale House Publishers and Grand Rapids, MI: Zondervan Publishing House, 1991.

McDowell, Josh, and Wilson, Bill, *A Ready Defense*, San Bernardino, CA: Here's Life Publishers, Inc., 1990.*

Muncaster, Ralph O., *Are There Hidden Codes in the Bible?* Eugene, OR: Harvest House, 2000.*

Muncaster, Ralph O., *How Can We Know for Certain We Are Going to Heaven?* Eugene, OR: Harvest House, 2000.*

Muncaster, Ralph O., *How Do We Know Jesus Is God?* Eugene, OR: Harvest House, 2000.*

Muncaster, Ralph O., *Is the Bible Really a Message from God?* Eugene, OR: Harvest House, 2000.*

Muncaster, Ralph O., *What Really Happened Christmas Morning?* Eugene, OR: Harvest House, 2000.*

Smith, F. LaGard, *The Daily Bible in Chronological Order*, Eugene, OR: Harvest House, 1984.

Walvoord, John F., *The Prophecy Knowledge Handbook*, Wheaton, IL: Victor Books, 1990.